Wild West Lawmen and Outlaws

Ryan P. Randolph

The Rosen Publishing Group's

PowerKids Press™

New York

Published in 2003 by The Rosen Publishing Group, Inc.
29 East 21st Street, New York, NY 10010

First Edition

Managing Editor: Kathy Kuhtz Campbell
Book Designer: Emily Muschinske

Photo Credits: Cover and title page (Wyatt Earp) courtesy the Craig Fouts Collection; cover and title page, 9, 10, 17 (bottom) © CORBIS; back cover, pp. 17 (top left), 20 courtesy George Stumpf, Deputy U.S. Marshal, (Ret); pp. 5 (top and bottom left), 6, 9 (left and right), 14, 18 (bottom), 21 © Bettmann/CORBIS; p. 5 (bottom right) © Jonathan Blair/CORBIS; p. 5 (top right) © The Everett Collection; pp. 6 (inset), 17 (top right) courtesy Arizona Historical Society/Tuscon; p. 10 (left) © Underwood and Underwood/CORBIS; p. 13 © Oklahoma Historical Society; p. 18 (right) Collection of R. G. McCubbin.

Randolph, Ryan P.
     Wild West lawmen and outlaws / Ryan P. Randolph.
          p. cm. — (The library of the westward expansion)
     Includes bibliographical references and index.
     Contents: Why was the West so wild? — Honor and the code of the West — Cattle rustling and cattle wars — Bank robbery — Women outlaws — Train robbing — The law of the West — Local lawmen and the posse — U.S. marshals, rangers, and detectives — The legacy of the Wild West.
     ISBN 0-8239-6293-8 (lib.)
     1. Frontier and pioneer life—West (U.S.)—Juvenile literature. 2. Outlaws—West (U.S.)—Biography—Juvenile literature. 3. Peace officers—West (U.S.)—Biography—Juvenile literature. 4. Violence—West (U.S.)—History—19th century—Juvenile literature. 5. West (U.S.)—Biography—Juvenile literature. 6. West (U.S.)—History—19th century—Juvenile literature. [1. Peace officers. 2. Robbers and outlaws. 3. West (U.S.)—History—19th century.] I. Title. II. Series.
     F596 .R359 2002   2001-005548
     978'.02'0922—dc21

Contents

Why Was the West So Wild?

We have all read stories and seen movies about the Wild West. When we think of the West we think of guns blazing, trains and banks being robbed, and outlaws and lawmen fighting. Why was the settlement of the western **frontier** of the United States so wild?

In the 1840s, white settlers moved from the eastern United States to the West and often settled in areas where police and courts did not exist. The settlers used guns for protection from outlaws and unfriendly Native Americans, and for hunting animals. Guns became a deadly tool for settling disagreements. They also made it easy for outlaws to rob wagons, trains, and banks. The American **Civil War** (1861–1865) added to the violence and lawlessness. Northern and Southern supporters lived in the same towns west of the Mississippi River. Conflict increased as former soldiers from both sides of the war drifted to the West.

Left: *Jesse James started out robbing banks and then robbed trains. Later people enjoyed reading about his crimes in dime novels (bottom left). Bottom Right: Butch Cassidy was a cattle rustler and bank robber.*

Top Right: *The 1969 movie Butch Cassidy and the Sundance Kid made Butch seem like he was not dangerous.*

Honor and the Code of the West

As more people moved to the West and settled the land, towns sprang up overnight. People developed a certain way of life, sometimes called the **code**, or law, of the West. The code of the West said that wrongs others made against you must be **avenged**. This way of life revolved around honor. People defended their honor by using guns and violence, or harmful physical force.

To cut down on the number of gunfights in many towns, the townspeople in these places passed laws that made it **illegal** to carry guns in the towns. In America's West during the mid-1800s, people did not consider it honorable to shoot an unarmed man.

The West was a wild place. It was hard to control outlaws because lawmen had to travel long distances to find and arrest them. Inset: This Colt revolver belonged to Deputy Marshal Wyatt Earp.

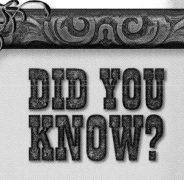

DID YOU KNOW?

The most popular guns in the West were Colt revolvers and Winchester rifles. The most popular Colt revolver was known as the Peacemaker. The 1873 Winchester 15-shot rifle was known as the gun that won the West.

Cattle Rustlers and Cattle Wars

The big business of cattle ranching helped the West's expansion. Ranchers hired cowboys and **gunmen** to drive huge herds of cattle. However, these gunmen were not necessarily **upstanding** citizens. The hard, lonely life of raising cattle attracted outlaws. Many cowboys became cattle **rustlers**, or thieves. They could sell stolen cattle for a profit or could start their own small ranches with the stolen cattle. Billy the Kid was one such gunman.

In 1878, William H. Bonney, known as Billy the Kid, became involved in New Mexico's Lincoln County War. Men who worked for L. G. Murphy murdered Billy's boss, John Tunstall, starting the war. Murphy was Tunstall's **rival**. To get even with Murphy, Billy killed many of those who he believed were responsible for his boss's death. In 1881, former buffalo hunter Pat Garrett formed a **posse** that hunted down and killed Billy.

Right: Cowboys worked with cattle on ranches, such as this one in Rita Blanco Canyon in Oklahoma. Far Right: Outlaw Billy the Kid was one of the most famous cattle rustlers in the Wild West. Top Left: A "Wanted" poster announces a large reward for Billy's capture.

REWARD
($5,000.00)
Reward for the capture, dead or alive,
of one Wm. Wright, better known as
"BILLY THE KID"

Age, 18. Height, 5 feet, 3 inches.
Weight, 125 lbs. Light hair, blue
eyes and even features. He is
the leader of the worst band of
desperadoes the Territory has
ever had to deal with. The above
reward will be paid for his capture
or positive proof of his death.

JIM. DALTON, Sheriff.

DEAD OR ALIVE!
"BILLY THE KID"

$5,000.00 REWARD

Wanted by the State of Missouri

JESSE & FRANK JAMES

For Train Robbery

Notify AUTHORITIES LIBERTY, MISSOURI

Above: Missouri offered a reward for the capture of brothers Jesse and Frank James. Right: Jesse and Frank James, seated, and Cole and Bob Younger, standing, formed a gang. In 1876, they tried to rob a bank in Minnesota but failed. The Younger brothers were wounded in the attempt.

Bank Robbers

Robbing banks was a quick but dangerous way for outlaws to steal money. The most famous Wild West bank robber was Jesse James. In 1866, brothers Jesse and Frank James and Cole Younger and his brothers robbed their first bank together in Liberty, Missouri. The James-Younger gang was involved in various bank and train robberies until 1882, when Bob Ford shot Jesse James.

The Dalton brothers and Bill Doolin took over where the James-Younger gang left off. The Dalton gang's last bank robbery ended in failure in 1892. Bill Doolin was not at this failed robbery. Doolin went on to start his own gang, robbing banks and wagons until famous lawman Bill Tilghman caught him in 1895.

DID YOU KNOW?

Henry Starr, called the Cherokee Badman, was the nephew of Bandit Queen Belle Starr. He began robbing banks in 1893 by using horses. By 1916, he had begun to use an automobile for his getaways, the first bank robber to do so.

Women Outlaws

For the most part, women took some of the wildness out of the Wild West. One reason for the calming effect of women was that women and men often settled down and had families. Women outlaws were not that common, but they did exist.

The most famous woman outlaw was Belle Starr. She has been linked to the James-Younger gang because, at one time, she was Cole Younger's **common-law** wife. During the 1880s, Starr was involved in stealing horses and cattle rustling. In 1883, she became one of the first women arrested and jailed for stealing horses. Belle Starr's life ended terribly, though. One story has it that in 1889, Starr's own son shot her in the back while she appeared in court.

In 1848, Myra Belle Shirley was born near Carthage, Missouri. Myra grew up to be Belle Starr, the Bandit Queen. Her home in Oklahoma became a hideout for other outlaws.

Train Robbers

After the **transcontinental** railroad connected the eastern and western United States in 1869, many more railroads spread westward. These railroads opened the West to settlers. They also became targets for organized gangs.

One well-known gang was the Wild Bunch. The Wild Bunch included Harvey "Kid Curry" Logan and his brothers, Tom "Black Jack" Ketchum and Harry "Sundance Kid" Longabaugh. They were led by Robert "Butch Cassidy" Parker. The Wild Bunch robbed trains, mine **payrolls**, and banks between 1896 and 1901. Most members of the Wild Bunch were either captured or killed.

Around 1900, Wild Bunch outlaws Harry Longabaugh, Will Carver, Ben Kilpatrick, Harvey Logan, and Robert Parker posed for a photographer.

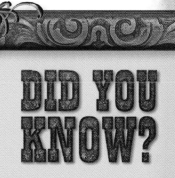

DID YOU KNOW?

Butch Cassidy and the Sundance Kid escaped to South America in 1902. There are two stories about how their lives ended. One says they were killed in Bolivia in 1909, the other says they came back to the United States and lived there until they died.

The Law of the West

Towns that did not have police forces often hired a sheriff to protect the people who lived there. The sheriff was free to make anyone his **deputy**, to collect taxes, and to raise a posse. The backgrounds of the sheriff and his deputies were sometimes questionable. Professional "peace officers," or lawmen, such as Wyatt Earp, often traveled from town to town as sheriffs.

Western towns did not have judges or courts in the late 1800s. The townspeople usually developed their own laws and systems of justice. Often the "judges" they hired had no legal experience. In one case, the man known as "Judge" Roy Bean set up the town court in his Langtry, Texas, **saloon**. In the 1880s and the 1890s, he called himself the Law West of the Pecos. He once fined a dead man $40 for having a hidden gun in his pocket.

Below: An 1893 photo shows Judge Roy Bean (seventh from left), "the law West of the Pecos," outside his saloon in Langtry, Texas. Right: Wyatt Earp served as a lawman in Wichita and Dodge City, Kansas, and in Tombstone, Arizona. Left: In Dodge City, Wyatt Earp wore the badge of a deputy U.S. marshal.

DEPUTY U.S. MARSHAL

Right: William "Bat" Masterson was a gambler, saloonkeeper, newspaperman, and lawman in Dodge City. As county sheriff and, later, as deputy U.S. marshal, he led many posses. Below: The posse organized to track the Wild Bunch poses in front of a Union Pacific Railroad car.

Local Lawmen and the Posse

It was dangerous to be a lawman. Cowboys and outlaws were always looking for a fight. William Barclay "Bat" Masterson and Wyatt Earp are the best-known lawmen of the Wild West. In 1879, Earp moved to Tombstone, Arizona, to join his brother, Virgil, a deputy U.S. marshal. Tombstone was where the Earp brothers and John Henry "Doc" Holliday shot several men in a gunfight on October 26, 1881, near the O.K. Corral.

In the West, outlaws often had to run from the sheriff and an eager posse of ordinary citizens. The posses chased, tracked down, and captured outlaws. Most Western posses earned respect for their efforts in finding those who broke the law.

DID YOU KNOW?

Movies often show two gunfighters walking 10 paces away from each other, turning, and "drawing" their guns. This kind of showdown was very rare in the real West. Shootings were often at close range without any warning.

U.S. Marshals, Texas Rangers, and Pinkerton Detectives

MARSHAL

Wearing the badge of U.S. marshal, Evett Nix led a group of eager deputies.

The law of the West became more organized after the Civil War. In 1875, Isaac Parker became the federal judge of the Western territories. He sentenced so many men to hang that he became known as the Hanging Judge. In 1893, Evett Nix was appointed the U.S. marshal of the Oklahoma (or Indian) Territory. He assembled a group of famous crime-fighting deputies, including Bill Tilghman.

Texas Rangers and Pinkerton detectives also fought crime on the western frontier. The Texas Rangers settled the range wars being fought by Texas cattle ranchers and prevented cattle rustling along the Texas-Mexico border. Railroad companies, ranchers, and mine operators hired Pinkerton detectives to capture train robbers, outlaws, and troublemakers.

Pinkerton's National Detective Agency.

FOUNDED BY ALLAN PINKERTON, 1850.

OFFICES.

ROBT. A. PINKERTON, New York,) Principals.
WM. A. PINKERTON, Chicago,)

GEO. D. BANGS.
General Manager, New York.
ALLAN PINKERTON,
Assistant General Manager,
New York.

JOHN CORNISH, Gen'l Sup't., Eastern Division, New York.
EDWARD S. GAYLOR, Gen'l Sup't., Middle Division, Chicago.
JAMES McPARLAND, Gen'l Supt., Western Division, Denver.

Attorneys: GUTHRIE, CRAVATH & HENDERSON,
New York.

TELEPHONE CONNECTION.

DENVER, OPERA HOUSE BLOCK.
J. C. FRASER, Supt.
NEW YORK. 57 BROADWAY
BOSTON, 30 COURT STREET
PHILADELPHIA, 441 CHESTNUT STREET
MONTREAL, MERCHANTS BANK BUILDING.
CHICAGO, 201 FIFTH AVENUE.
ST. PAUL, GERMANIA BANK BUILDING.
ST. LOUIS, WAINWRIGHT BUILDING.
KANSAS CITY, 622 MAIN STREET.
PORTLAND, ORE. MARQUAM BLOCK.
SEATTLE, WASH. BAILEY BLOCK.
SAN FRANCISCO, CROCKER BUILDING.

REPRESENTING THE AMERICAN BANKERS' ASSOCIATION.

$4,000.00 REWARD.

CIRCULAR No. 2.

DENVER, Colo., January 24th, 1902.

THE FIRST NATIONAL BANK OF WINNEMUCCA, Nevada, a member of THE AMERICAN BANKERS' ASSOCIATION, was robbed of $32,640 at the noon hour, September 19th, 1900, by three men who entered the bank and "held up" the cashier and four other persons. Two of the robbers carried revolvers and a third a Winchester rifle. They compelled the five persons to go into the inner office of the bank while the robbery was committed.

At least $31,000 was in $20 gold coin; $1,200 in $5 and $10 gold coin; the balance in currency, including one $50 bill.

Since the issuance of our first circular, dated Denver, Colo., May 15th, 1901, it has been positively determined that two of the men who committed this robbery were:

1. GEORGE PARKER, alias "BUTCH" CASSIDY, alias GEORGE CASSIDY, alias INGERFIELD.
2. HARRY LONGBAUGH, alias "KID" LONGBAUGH, alias HARRY ALONZO, alias "THE SUNDANCE KID;"

PARKER and LONGBAUGH are members of the HARVEY LOGAN alias "KID" CURRY band of bank and train (express) "hold up" robbers.

For the arrest, detention and surrender to an authorized officer of the State of Nevada of each or any one of the men who robbed the FIRST NATIONAL BANK OF WINNEMUCCA, the following rewards are offered:

BY THE FIRST NATIONAL BANK OF WINNEMUCCA: $1,000 for each robber.
Also 25 per cent. in proportionate shares, on all money recovered.

BY THE AMERICAN BANKERS' ASSOCIATION: $1,000 for each robber.
This reward to be paid on proper identification of either PARKER or LONGBAUGH.

Persons furnishing information leading to the arrest of either or all of the robbers will be entitled to share in the reward.

The outlaws, whose photographs, descriptions and histories appear on this circular MAY ATTEMPT TO CIRCULATE or be in possession of the following described NEW INCOMPLETE BANK NOTES of the NATIONAL BANK OF MONTANA and THE AMERICAN NATIONAL BANK, both of HELENA, MONT., which were stolen by members of the HARVEY LOGAN, alias "KID" CURRY BAND, from the GREAT NORTHERN (RAILWAY) EXPRESS No. 3, near Wagner, Mont., July 3rd, 1901, by "hold up" methods.

$40,000. INCOMPLETE NEW BANK NOTES of the NATIONAL BANK OF MONTANA (Helena, Montana), $24,000 of which was in ten dollar bills and $16,000 of which was in twenty dollar bills.

Serial Number 1201 to 2000 inclusive;

Below appear the photographs, descriptions and histories of GEORGE PARKER, alias "BUTCH CASSIDY, alias GEORGE CASSIDY, alias INGERFIELD and HARRY LONGBAUGH alias HARRY ALONZO.

GEORGE PARKER.
First photograph taken July 15, 1894.

GEORGE PARKER.
Last photograph taken Nov. 21, 1900.

Name..George Parker, alias "Butch" Cassidy, alias George Cassidy, alias Ingerfield.
Nationality...................American
Occupation................Cowboy; rustler
Criminal Occupation......Bank robber and highwayman, cattle and horse thief
Age..36 yrs. (1901)...Height...5 feet 9 in
Weight..165 lbs......Build.....Medium
Complexion..Light..Color of Hair..Flaxen
Eyes.....Blue......Mustache..Sandy, if any
Remarks:—Two cut scars back of head, small scar under left eye, small brown mole calf of leg. "Butch" Cassidy is known as a criminal principally in Wyoming, Utah, Idaho, Colorado and Nevada and has served time in Wyoming State penitentiary at Laramie for grand larceny, but was pardoned January 19th, 1896.

HARRY LONGBAUGH.
Photograph taken Nov. 21, 1900.

Name..Harry Longbaugh, alias "Kid" Longbaugh, alias Harry Alonzo alias Frank Jones, alias Frank Boyd, alias the "Sundance Kid"
Nationality....Swedish-American..Occupation....Cowboy; rustler
Criminal Occupation.......Highwayman, bank burglar, cattle and horse thief
Age...........35 years.......Height..........5 feet 10 in
Weight......165 to 175 lbs......Build.........Good
Eyes.......Blue or gray.........Complexion........Medium
Mustache or Beard...........(if any), natural color brown, reddish tinge
Features.......Grecian type....Nose........Rather long
Color of Hair.....Natural color brown, may be dyed; combs it pompadour.
IS BOW-LEGGED AND HIS FEET FAR APART.
Remarks:—Harry Longbaugh served 18 months in jail at Sundance, Cook Co., Wyoming, when a boy, for horse stealing. In December, 1892, Harry Longbaugh, Bill Madden and Henry Bass "held up" a Great Northern train at Malta, Montana. Bass and Madden were tried for this crime, convicted and sentenced to 10 and 14 years respectively; Longbaugh escaped and since has been a fugitive. June 28, 1897, under the name of Frank Jones, Longbaugh participated with Harvey Logan, alias Curry, Tom Day and Walter Putney, in the Belle Fourche, South Dakota, bank robbery. All were arrested, but Longbaugh and Harvey Logan escaped from jail at Deadwood, October 31, the same year. Longbaugh has not since been arrested.

We also publish below a photograph, history and description of CAMILLA HANKS, alias O. C. HANKS, alias CHARLEY JONES, alias "DEAF" CHARLEY, who may be found in the company of either PARKER, alias CASSIDY or LONGBAUGH, alias ALONZO, and for whom a proportionate amount of a $5,000.00 Reward is offered by the GREAT NORTHERN EXPRESS COMPANY upon arrest and conviction for participation in the Great Northern (Railway) Express robbery near Wagner, Mont., July 3rd, 1901.

Name..O. C. Hanks, alias Camilla Hanks, alias Charley Jones, alias Deaf Charley.
Nationality.... American ....Occupation...........Cowboy
Criminal Occupation ....Train robber; an ex-convict
Age............38 years (1901)......Height..............5 feet 10 in
Weight.........156 lbs.......Build.............Good
Complexion......Sandy......Color of Hair..........Auburn
Eyes........Blue..........Mustache or Beard......(if any), natural color sandy
Remarks:—Scar from burn, size 25c piece, on right forearm. Small scar right leg, above ankle. Mole near right nipple. Leans his head slightly to the left. Somewhat deaf. Raised at Yorktown, Texas, fugitive from there charged with rape; also wanted in New Mexico on charge of murder. Arrested in Teton County, Montana, 1892, and sentenced to 10 years in the penitentiary at Deer Lodge, for holding up Northern Pacific train near Big Timber, Montana. Released April 30th, 1901.

CAMILLA HANKS.

HARVEY LOGAN, alias "KID" CURRY, referred to in our first circular issued from Denver on May 15, 1901, is now under arrest.

BEN KILPATRICK, alias JOHN ARNOLD, alias "THE TALL TEXAN" of Concho County, Texas, another member of the Harvey Logan band of outlaws, was arrested at St. Louis, Mo., on November 5th, 1901, tried, convicted and sentenced to 15 years for participation in the robbery of the GREAT NORTHERN EXPRESS COMPANY, near Wagner, Mont.

WILLIAM CARVER, alias "BILL" CARVER, of Sonora, Sutton County, Texas, another member of this band, was killed April 2nd, 1901, by Sheriff E. S. Bryant, while resisting arrest on charge of murder.

IN CASE OF AN ARREST immediately notify PINKERTON'S NATIONAL DETECTIVE AGENCY at the above listed offices.

Pinkerton's National Detective Agency,
Opera House Block, Denver, Colo.

J. C. FRASER,
Resident Sup't., DENVER, COLO.

Give this circular to the police of their city or district.

...War-hal, Constable, Sheriff or Deputy or a Peace officer.

Pinkerton's National Detective Agency.

FOUNDED BY ALLAN PINKERTON, 1850.

OFFICES.

ROBT. A. PINKERTON, New York,) Principals.
WM. A. PINKERTON, Chicago,)

GEO. D. BANGS.
General Manager, New York.
ALLAN PINKERTON,
Assistant General Manager,
New York.

JOHN CORNISH, Gen'l Sup't., Eastern Division, New York.
EDWARD S. GAYLOR, Gen'l Sup't., Middle Division, Chicago.
JAMES McPARLAND, Gen'l Sup't., Western Division, Denver.

Attorneys:— GUTHRIE, CRAVATH & HENDERSON,
New York.

TELEPHONE CONNECTION.

DENVER, OPERA HOUSE BLOCK
J. C. FRASER, Supt.
NEW YORK. 57 BROADWAY
BOSTON, 30 COURT STREET
PHILADELPHIA, 441 CHESTNUT STREET
MONTREAL, MERCHANTS BANK BUILDING.
CHICAGO, 201 FIFTH AVENUE.
ST. PAUL, GERMANIA BANK BUILDING.
ST. LOUIS, WAINWRIGHT BUILDING.
KANSAS CITY, 622 MAIN STREET.
PORTLAND, ORE. MARQUAM BLOCK.
SEATTLE, WASH. BAILEY BLOCK.
SAN FRANCISCO, CROCKER BUILDING.

REPRESENTING THE AMERICAN BANKERS' ASSOCIATION.

$4,000.00 REWARD.

Pinkerton's National Detective Agency was created in 1850 to solve train and bank robberies.
Inset: A detail shows the agency's $4,000 award offer for capturing the Wild Bunch.

The Legacy of the Wild West

The wildness of the West started to disappear in the late 1800s. With the growing number of people moving into and settling the western territories came formal police forces and courts.

Even after the Wild West was tamed, its **legend** lived on. In the 1880s, Wild West shows and rodeos became popular. William "Buffalo Bill" Cody ran the most famous Wild West show, which included shooting matches with Annie Oakley. It toured the eastern region of the United States and parts of Europe. When Wild West shows became less popular in the 1920s, rodeos continued some cowboy acts, such as bronco riding. Even today's movies and books tell **idealized** stories of the Wild West, keeping those wild days alive for everyone around the world.

Glossary

avenged (uh-VENJD) Having gotten back at someone for a wrong done to oneself or another.

Civil War (SIH-vul WOR) 1. A war between two sides within one country. 2. The war fought between the Northern and Southern states of America from 1861 to 1865.

code (KOHD) A law or system of rules.

common-law (KAH-min-law) Having to do with a relationship between a man and a woman in which they live together a long time and, by law, become married.

deputy (DEP-yoo-tee) A second in command or an assistant that has the power to act to enforce the law.

frontier (frun-TEER) The edge of a settled country, where the wilderness begins.

gunmen (GUN-min) A group of men known for their speed and skill handling a gun.

idealized (eye-DEE-lyzd) Made to seem more romantic or better than something actually is; something existing in the imagination only.

illegal (ih-LEE-gul) Against the law.

legend (LEJ-end) A story passed down through the years that many people believe.

payrolls (PAY-rolz) The money to be paid to workers.

posse (PAH-see) A group of people gathered together by a lawman to help capture an outlaw.

rival (RY-vul) A person who is or tries to be as good or better than another.

rustlers (RUS-lurz) Thieves, especially those who steal animals from a farm or a ranch.

saloon (suh-LOON) A combination restaurant, bar, and gaming place. It often provided rooms for guests, and poker games.

transcontinental (tranz-kon-tin-EN-tul) Going across a continent.

upstanding (up-STAND-ing) Law-abiding; marked by honesty.

Index

Primary Sources

Page 5 (top). *Jesse James*. This photograph from the 1860s is one of the few existing today of the famous outlaw. **Page 5 (bottom)**. *Butch Cassidy*. Date unknown. Cassidy was photographed by Jonathan Blair while Cassidy was a prisoner in Wyoming State Penitentiary. **Page 6 (inset)**. *Colt Single Action Army revolver*. This 1883 revolver was owned by Wyatt Earp while he worked in Tombstone, Arizona. Samuel Colt invented the first practical revolver in 1836, and he made the guns in Hartford, Connecticut. **Page 9 (far right)**. *Billy the Kid*. This ferrotype, or tintype, makes it appear as though Billy was left-handed because it is viewed from the back. The error about his being left-handed has been kept alive for more than 100 years. **Page 13**. *Belle Starr*. This photograph was taken by Roeder on May 24, 1886, at Fort Smith, Arkansas. **Page 14**. *The Hole-in-the-Wall Gang, also called the Wild Bunch*. This photograph was taken in 1900 by Noah H. Rose. The Hole-in-the-Wall was the name of the Wild Bunch's hideout in Wyoming. Today the photo is in the collection of the Western History and Genealogy Department of the Denver Public Library, Denver, Colorado. **Page 17 (bottom)**. *Judge Roy Bean's saloon-courthouse*. This photo was taken on February 21, 1893, and shows Bean and other "lawmen" in front of the Jersey Lilly Saloon in Langtry, Texas. Bean named his saloon and the town in Texas after the English actress Lillie Langtry. **Page 17 and Page 20**. Deputy U.S. Marshal and Marshal badges. Usually the badge of highest rank (U.S. marshal) was the simplest in design. **Page 18 (top)**. *Bat Masterson in Dodge City, Kansas*. This photograph was taken in 1885. It is from the collection of Robert G. McCubbin, Santa Fe, New Mexico.

Web Sites

To learn more about Wild West lawmen and outlaws, check out these Web sites:

http://history.cc.ukans.edu/heritage/research/gunfighters.html
www.nmsu.edu/~redtt/Resources/html/Outlaws.html
www.jessejamesvirtualmuseum.com/

Mig the Pig

Colin and
Jacqui Hawkins

G. P. Putnam's Sons   New York

Do you know Mig the pig?

Mig the pig is very big.

She likes to wear a bright red wig.

W

Mig often goes riding in her gig.

One day while out in her gig,
Mig stopped for a dig.

d

But the wind blew her red wig onto a twig.

Mig shook the twig and down came her wig along with a fig.

So happy was Mig to get back her red wig, along with a fig that she danced a wild jig.

What will Mig

...do with her fig?

Then home in the gig to bake the fig went the pig called Mig.